YOUR KNOWLEDGE HAS VALUE

- We will publish your bachelor's and master's thesis, essays and papers

- Your own eBook and book - sold worldwide in all relevant shops

- Earn money with each sale

Upload your text at www.GRIN.com
and publish for free

Gesa Biermann

Stereotypes Galore! Women's Emancipation as Reflected in Advertising

GRIN Verlag

Bibliografische Information der Deutschen Nationalbibliothek:

Die Deutsche Bibliothek verzeichnet diese Publikation in der Deutschen National-
bibliografie; detaillierte bibliografische Daten sind im Internet über http://dnb.d-
nb.de/ abrufbar.

Imprint:

Copyright © 2009 GRIN Verlag GmbH
Druck und Bindung: Books on Demand GmbH, Norderstedt Germany
ISBN: 978-3-640-80278-4

This book at GRIN:

http://www.grin.com/en/e-book/164821/stereotypes-galore-women-s-emancipation-
as-reflected-in-advertising

Maria-Ward-Gymnasium Nymphenburg
der Erzdiözese München und Freising

Abiturjahrgang 2009

FACHARBEIT

Stereotypes Galore! Women's Emancipation as Reflected in Advertising

Verfasserin: **Gesa Biermann**

Leistungskurs: **Englisch**
Kursleiter:

Abgabetermin: **30. Januar 2009**

Table of Contents

I. Introduction

A woman rushes across the screen, cleaning the floor with the latest "turbo power 3" multifunction vacuum cleaner, feeds her baby with the new and improved baby formula and marvels at her almost blindingly clean dishes, then turns to the camera with a smile on her face that suggests she could not imagine a more satisfying life. This description might sound a little old fashioned and restricting, but it is commonly conveyed to us through advertising, even today. Is this truly the concept we have of modern women? Has not the women's movement brought about more change than just in legal status? As advertising is one of the most powerful educational mediums in modern society, the image of women it conveys is not only quite interesting, but also of great importance. There is such an overload of advertising surrounding us; we're bombarded daily with a vast amount on the radio, TV, online, on billboards, in magazines, even on the most common things like a pen—there is no way to escape its influence.

Advertising's key objective is making money; selling an image of perfection to consumers makes great business sense, because it sends people on a never-ending quest, trying to achieve the impossible, all the while spending endless amounts of money. Advertising does not only sell a product, but, through stereotyped characters, also provides us with an exemplary way of life. The concepts of beauty, love, and normalcy it promotes, might have changed in the course of 40 years, but the central message remains the same, "you have to buy this or otherwise you will be unacceptable".

It seems that in the 21st century, women's emancipation is an issue that should long since have been checked off the list as accomplished. Western society, especially the USA, land of unlimited opportunity, is one that believes in women's equality and ability to accomplish anything man can, a society where gender stereotypes seem to be out of place, or so we like to think. The great effect of the feminist movement, with better educated, working women, participating in every aspect of life, is undeniable, yet the influence it has had on advertising's portrayal of women remains questionable. Have stereotypes been banished, did they evolved or maybe even stay the same? The focus is on the 1950s and the 1990s as representative decades for the pre-and post-feminist attitudes, in order to explore the truth of advertising and finally be able to answer the question: does advertising's image of women match their place in society?

II. Women's Position in Society: American Social History

1. First-Wave Feminism: Women Gain the Right to Vote

If in 1776, the First Lady of the United States acknowledged the importance of including women in government matters, by telling her husband to "remember the ladies"[1] in his drafting of new laws, why did it take another 144 years for her suggestion to be put into action? It is obvious that feminist ideas were present, but the ideals set for women before the first wave of feminism showed a very different reality. The social circumstances gave cause to formulate the basic four principles of true womanhood as: "piety, purity, domesticity, and submissiveness"[2]. Limited education was the norm, which meant only a few years of schooling, instruction centered on teaching women how to be a good homemaker, in the end leaving them with slim chances of finding work. The one respectable goal in life for a woman was to get married, after which she would loose her legal identity and therefore any minimal rights she had before. Those were the conditions for middle-class white women; women of lower education were expected to work, but could only get a position in low-paying jobs, such as domestic service, while black women were mostly slaves and therefore not even viewed as citizens[3].

What women of all economic and racial background had in common, however, was disenfranchisement, not being able to vote, and therefore no representation in the legislature. They began to question their social status; but just how did the women's movement begin? Well, "surprisingly often, change began with half a dozen women, sitting around a kitchen table, defining a problem and figuring out what they could do about it"[4]. Such a spontaneous campaign also marked the official beginning of the women's movement: the Seneca Falls Convention in 1848. Organized by Lucretia Mott and Elizabeth Cady Stanton, the purpose of the conference was to discuss the "social, civil, and religious rights of woman"[5]. They drafted a Declaration of Sentiments, modeled after the Declaration of Independence, to provide a focal point for the meeting. In their opening remarks, they declared that "all men and women are created

---

[1] "Letter from Abigail Adams to John Adams, 31 March – April 1776", Adams Family Papers: An Electronic Archive, *Massachusetts Historical Society*, 18 December 2008.
<http://www.masshist.org/digitaladams/aea/cfm/doc.cfm?id=L17760331aa>.
[2] see: Dicker, R., A History of U.S. Feminisms, Seal Press, Berkeley, California 2008, p. 21.
[3] see: ibid., p. 21-24.
[4] Davis, F., Moving the Mountain: The Women's Movement in America since 1960, Touchstone, New York 1991, p. 9.
[5] Stanton, E. and Mott, L. "The First Convention Ever Called to Discuss the Civil and Political Rights of Women, Seneca Falls, N.Y., July 19, 20, 1848", National American Woman Suffrage Association Collection, *Library of Congress,* 25 December 2008.
<http://www.hdl.loc.gov/loc.rbc/rbnawsa.n7548>.

equal"[6], thereby setting the tone for the meeting. They presented the hardships women had to face in American society and managed to pass resolutions ensuring women's equality in "education, inheritance, property rights, divorce, and child custody"[7]. Only the claim of suffrage remained unanswered.

At the outset of the women's movement, it was interlaced with other movements of reform, most notably the abolitionist movement. The leaders of these, at the beginning, small organizations, soon realized that "disenfranchisement severely hampered reformatory efforts"[8]. But skeptics of the vote for women, not only feared that it would be a setback for colored men, who were also campaigning for the same cause, but were also worried that illiterate women of color would claim their right to vote. A separate movement for women's suffrage followed, consisting mostly of White, middle class, well-educated women. These suffragists did not give up on the vote for women and also kept on confronting stereotypes, such as the "cult of domesticity"[9], which saw women as a servant to her husband and caretaker of her children, in the home, exclusively. The act of women campaigning in public was in itself a protest against the norm that "respectable women did not exit the private sphere of the home to put themselves forward and speak out in mixed company"[10]. Prejudice against the movement was further advanced by the common belief that women "have smaller brains of inferior quality to men's"[11].

After the first convention at Seneca Falls, a meeting was held every year between 1850 and 1860, to further advance women's rights and fight for suffrage. The Civil War put a damper on activism, however, as many thought it was simply not women's turn and promoted abolitionism instead. Women activists held high hopes that they would be rewarded for their service to the Union with a suffrage amendment. The end of the war did not bring the hoped-for reward, but only resulted in a division within the movement, as blacks were campaigning for the Fourteenth Amendment, which would only grant black men the right to vote. Different associations were formed, most notably the National American Woman Suffrage Association (NAWSA), who fought alongside each other for suffrage, either on state- or federal level. The first state to grant suffrage to women was Wyoming, in 1869, followed by Utah, Colorado and Idaho in the years 1870 to 1896. Then a long dry period followed; no new states granted suffrage until 1910.

[6] see: ibid.
[7] Ryan, B., Feminism and the Women's Movement, Routledge, New York 1992, p. 16.
[8] Kroløkke, C. and Sørensen, A., Gender Communication Theories & Analyses: From Silence to Performance, Sage Publications, Thousand Oaks, California 2006, p. 4.
[9] see: ibid., p. 5.
[10] Dicker, R., p. 28.
[11] Boham L. and Lipton, M., "Women Writing: 1890-Present", Yale-New Haven Teachers Institute 2008, 23 December 2008. <http://www.yale.edu/ynhti/curriculum/units/1978/3/78.03.09.x.html>.

At the turn of the century, the traditional role of women also came under fire, with Victoria Woodhull promoting sexual freedom and Margaret Sanger, who coined the term "birth control", declaring that "no woman can call herself free, who does not own and control her own body"[12]. By the early twentieth century, a new generation of suffrage activists had stepped on the scene, who called for more direct action, "advocating public demonstrations, parades, and picketing"[13]. In so doing, women raised attention to their cause more than ever before, and won over the sympathy of the public, when they were jailed for their commitment. In 1910, Washington State granted suffrage to women, thereby ending the fourteen-year dry period. Seven more states followed and the Nineteenth Amendment, securing the right to vote for women, was finally passed in 1920, after a 72-year struggle for suffrage[14].

2. Second-Wave Feminism: The Personal Becomes Political

The term "women's liberation" quickly conjures up images of bra-burning, hysteric females in our minds. Fact is, no bras were ever burned during the second wave of feminism in the 1960s and 70s. The stereotypical image of a feminist was branded in our minds by overzealous media coverage of a demonstration at the Miss America Beauty Pageant, in 1968. Two hundred activists protested American society's beauty standards; they tossed, not burned, objects of feminine oppression, such as false eyelashes, high-heels, makeup, and bras into a "freedom trash can". Ironically, even 40 years later, the link between a "bra-burner" and a feminist persists.[15]

The resurgence of feminism in the 1960s leaves us with the question of what happened between the waves. Feminism did not die completely, as was strongly enforced by the media, which sought every piece of evidence pointing to its funeral. Fact is, after the vote was won, women did not crowd at the polling stations and it was concluded that suffrage was a failure and feminism no longer existed. However, many smaller activist groups emerged out of the larger ones that had fought for suffrage. They fought for birth control and the women's peace movement, but the women's movement itself was lacking a unified goal.[16] They got what they wanted in the postwar years of the 50s. During this period an effort was made to reestablish "'normalcy' [...] with men as

---

[12] Sochen, J., Movers and Shakers: American Women Thinkers and Activists 1900-1970, Quadrangle, New York 1973, p. 105.
[13] Dicker, R., p. 47.
[14] see ibid., p. 30-55.
[15] see: Berkeley, K., The Women's Liberation Movement in America, Greenwood Press, Westport, Connecticut 1999, p. 3-4.
[16] see: Davis, F., p. 26-28.

breadwinners and women as homemakers"[17], as gender-based roles in society had been reversed during World War II, when many women had become part of the workforce. Now the role as stay-at-home wife and mother was pressed onto women as the ideal way of life once more. Magazines, teaching women how to do everything "just perfect", from cooking to doing laundry and raising children, are the prime example of the inescapable pressure put on women.[18] The problems of the suburban housewife were strange to black women and men, however, who faced racial discrimination and segregation. The Civil Rights Movement developed out of black activism in the South and acts as the forerunner to the 1960s feminist movement.[19] A parallel can be seen between the first and second wave of feminism, as both sprung up in a social climate conducive to reform and developed out of movements for black rights.

As women joined in to advocate blacks' rights and demonstrate in the anti-Vietnam War movement, they once again found themselves reduced to doing paperwork, excluded from any assertive action.[20] Aside from the sexism women had to face in these social movements, they had to overcome many other obstacles in their daily lives:

> At midcentury, women were limited in the courses they could take in high school; discouraged from considering any but the most traditional, feminine careers; kept out of graduate schools, medical schools, and law schools by quotas; barred from many occupations; automatically fired when they became pregnant; routinely denied credit; and forbidden by law to sit on juries in some states. Most Americans, male and female, took it for granted that as breadwinners, men had a right to earn more than a woman who was doing the same job. Battered wives had nowhere to turn; sexual harassment was a dirty secret; abortion was illegal; and a woman who was raped had to produce a witness if she wanted the rapist brought to justice.[21]

Once again women saw the need for a separate movement for their own rights. They formulated their key demands as: "the right to safe and legal abortion, the right to accessible and affordable childcare, and equal opportunities in education and employment".[22] Typical of the women's liberation movement was its dissonance concerning tactic and root cause. Was male supremacy or capitalism to blame? Would direct action or "consciousness raising", in the form of small group discussion, be more effective?[23] A member of such a "consciousness-raising" group coined the phrase "the

---

[17] Dicker, R., p. 64-65.
[18] see: ibid., p. 65.
[19] Ryan, B., p. 42.
[20] see: Kroløkke, C. and Sørensen, A., p. 8-9.
[21] Davis, F., p. 491.
[22] see: Dicker, R., p. 58.
[23] Berkeley, K., p. 44.

personal is political", meaning that problems in the private home could only be helped by changing society at large, which became the central idea of the second wave.[24]

As much as the movement differed in tactic, it was lacking diversity in the form of race and sexual orientation. Even the mainstream organization National Organization for Women (NOW) had to cope with internal divisions, especially where interracial dialogue fell short.[25] Black women recognized the existence of sexism, but felt the struggle against racism was more urgent. The fear of white women, that their black sisters would ridicule their claims of oppression, further prevented a joint movement.[26] Lesbianism presents the second split; many women's organizations were concerned that their projects would not be taken seriously if associated with homosexuality. Sadly, the common goal of not wanting to be discriminated against based on sex or sexual orientation, was often overlooked, much to the devastation of the women's movement in the 1970s, as it experienced a gay-straight split.[27]

Even though the many strains of the movement worked mostly separately, fast results were achieved through NOW. The Equal Pay Act was passed in 1963; Title VII of the Civil Rights Act, which forbade discrimination at the workplace on the basis of sex, race, color, or national origin, was signed into law in 1964.[28] Aside from the fast successes, the second-wave feminists failed in their quest to get the Equal Rights Amendment, which states "equality of rights under the law shall not be denied or abridged by the United States or any state on the account of sex"[29], signed into law. First introduced to Congress by Alice Paul in 1923, it was not ratified by enough states in time for its deadline. The loss of the ERA struck a blow to the movement, as it once again lost its unifying goal.[30] Many of the changes women of the second wave accomplished were through new laws and legislation, but maybe even more significant were the personal advances they made. Through the new sense of sisterhood, women found the strength to be affirmative and take charge of their own lives, changing the atmosphere in their homes, at work and gaining the confidence to believe in their own strength of character[31] to break the "glass ceiling", an invisible blockade which had been keeping them from climbing the career ladder.[32]

---

[24] see: Dicker, R., p. 81.
[25] see: ibid., p. 71-74.
[26] see: Berkeley, K., p. 50-51.
[27] see: Dicker, R., p. 92-95.
[28] see: Berkeley, K., p. 25-29.
[29] Ryan, B., p. 166
[30] see: ibid., p. 108-109.
[31] Eisenberg, B. and Ruthsdotter, M., "Living the Legacy: The Women's Rights Movement 1848-1998", *National Women's History Project,* 28 December 2008. <http://www.legacy98.org/move-hist.html>.
[32] Dicker, R., p. 145.

3. Third-Wave Feminism: Finally Diversity

In spite of ample media coverage of feminism's death after the first and again, after the second wave, the ebb between the waves only seemed to be "the quiet before the storm" as feminist activism surged once again. After the defeat of the ERA, feminism was proclaimed dead once more in the 1980s and young women felt uncomfortable labeling themselves feminist, because of the negative connotation the term had received through media coverage. The backlash the movement experienced in the late 1970s is closely tied to the emergence of the New Right, which reemphasized family values, they claimed, had been destroyed by feminists. They linked feminist propaganda such as the ERA, the issue of abortion, homosexuality and equity in education, to the destruction of the American family.[33] It was the Clarence Thomas confirmation hearings in the 1990s, however, which finally caused feminists' patience to run out. When Thomas was nominated as Supreme Court justice, the media released claims of alleged sexual harassment. At the hearings that followed, the accuser, Anita Hill, was met with scorn and condescension, by the all-male Judiciary Committee. Thomas denied any accusations and was confirmed to his post by a narrow vote. This event once more mobilized feminist forces, as it made evident that women were simply not heard.[34]

The third wave of feminism developed in a very different direction than the second wave, becoming more global and inclusive of women of color and all social classes.[35] Multiplicity was the keyword, also in the range of issues covered; women now saw their oppression not as solely based on sex, they were also beginning to deal with economic oppression and environmental issues, concerns not traditionally considered to be "feminist". A feminism of many perspectives evolved; this simultaneously meant that the movement became more inclusive, accepting diversity, but also more subjective, challenging the idea of "universal womanhood". This new attitude was criticized as being self-absorbed and unpolitical, yet many feminist groups practiced quite a creative form of activism.[36] Among these was Riot Grrrl, an underground punk rock movement, whose members made their dissatisfaction heard through the lyrics of their songs. The countermovement to the aggressive Riot Grrrl was "girlie feminism". Women suddenly reclaimed everything feminine, wearing high-heels and lipstick, things that the "bra-burners" of the second wave would have linked with male oppression. Women now used these as assets, parading them in a parodic and playful way. By doing this, they

---

[33] see: Berkeley, K., p. 87-88.
[34] see: Dicker, R., p. 116-118.
[35] see: Davis, F., p. 494.
[36] see: Dicker, R., p. 126-129.

opposed the feminist stereotype and embraced femininity with a new confidence.[37] This extroverted, pro-sex attitude not only led to a more lighthearted approach of femininity, but ultimately also induced a questioning of beauty ideals. The unrealistic beauty ideals that are set for women are so restrictive and harmful[38] that "body image [...] may be the pivotal third wave issue—the common struggle that mobilizes the current feminist generation"[39].

The third wave of feminism is much more difficult to grasp than the first or second wave, because it is history in the making, which does not allow for an analysis in retrospect of the events. As old goals are accomplished, a new set of issues is ready to be dealt with, therefore, the race is not yet, and may never be, won. But there is a heritage of achievements of which to be proud. Maybe one of the most important legacies feminists have left is the immense research and teaching on women's issues[40], the awareness of oppression and a sense to prevent it. What was once an abstract feminist thought has become part of the widely accepted truth about women and equality.[41] However, in the twenty-first century, the need for feminism is still apparent, as for example, women in 2007 only earned 89 cents to a man's dollar[42].

III. Comparison of the Portrayal of Women in Advertising Campaigns of the 1950s and the 1990s:

1. The Power of Advertising

"Advertising, more than art, literature, or editorials, allows us to track our sociological history: the rise and fall of fads, crazes, and social movements; political issues of the times; changing interests and tastes in clothes, entertainment, vices, and food; and scenes of social life as they were lived."[43] If this is true, the three waves of feminism should have left a definite mark on advertising's portrayal of women. But did it really? Is advertising reflective of the rights women have gained and their new, equal status? In order to be able to answer this properly, an understanding of advertising's function and strategy is necessary. Advertising can be defined as: "The activity of attracting public

---

[37] see: ibid., p. 121-123.
[38] see: ibid., p. 141-142.
[39] ibid., p. 142.
[40] see: Kroløkke, C. and Sørensen, A., p. 15.
[41] Davis, F., p. 493.
[42] "Highlights of Women's Earnings in 2007", *U.S. Bureau of Labor Statistics* 2007, 16 January 2009. <http://www.bls.gov/cps/cpswom2007.pdf>.
[43] Cortese, A., Provocateur: Images of Women and Minorities in Advertising, Rowan & Littlefield Publishers, Inc., Lanham, Maryland 2008. p. 3.

attention to a product or business, as by paid announcements in the print, broadcast, or electronic media"[44], or in other words, advertising is a paid, widely spread means of persuasion. Advertising has the difficult job of trying to please everyone, it must "as a rule appeal to as large a section of the public as possible. And the focal point of this appeal can be only one thing: the product"[45]. It has to work with certain tools to market products to people; one of them is stereotyping. Stereotypes allow a person to assume a universal role that a wide range of people can relate to. In the short time an advertisement has to convey its message, the stereotype acts like a "code" to allow the audience to immediately understand the setting and role of the person portrayed, and therefore grasp the use of the product advertised.[46]

When trying to trace developments of the women's movement in advertising, a comparison of the 1950s and the 1990s is sensible, because this allows for a direct contrast of the conservative backlash during the 50s, before the second wave, and the accomplishments achieved through all three waves of feminism, as advertising from the 90s should depict. In the course of women's history, groundbreaking change in women's lives is evident, but the question remains, whether this undeniable shift in gender roles is also apparent in advertising.

2. In Search of Stereotypes: Advertising of the 1950s

The conservative era of the 1950s was characterized by reintroducing family values and the corresponding gender roles, the man as the breadwinner and the woman as the homemaker. "The suburban housewife" was enforced as "the dream of young American women"[47] by everything surrounding them: magazines, newspapers and books, television programs and finally, advertising. As most of the products advertised were related to housework or beauty, the number one target consumer were women.[48] In these, the feminine stereotype, what was proper behavior and etiquette for women, was reinforced. Women were portrayed as dependent, emotional, unassertive, passive, caring, and kind. This translates into the stereotype of the perfect wife and mother:

---

[44] "Advertising", Def. 1, *The American Heritage® Dictionary of the English Language*, 4th ed., Houghton Mifflin, Boston 2000, 10 January 2009. <http://www.bartleby.com/61/57/A0105700.html>.
[45] Barth, M., <u>Stark reduziert!,</u> Silke Schreiber Verlag, Heidenheim an der Brenz, Germany 2000, p. 185.
[46] see: "Media Stereotyping", *Media Awareness Network* 2009, 11 January 2009. <http://www.media-awareness.ca/english/issues/stereotyping/>.
[47] Berkeley, K., p. 153.
[48] see: Parkin, K., <u>Food Is Love: Food Advertising and Gender Roles in Modern America</u>, University of Pennsylvania Press, Philadelphia, Pennsylvania 2006. p. 12.

white, quiet and polished. Her universe was centered solely around home, husband and reputation.

While new ways of advertising, such as outdoor, radio and television commercials, had been introduced by 1950, print advertising remained the most important; in fact it remains the sector of the advertising industry that makes for over 50% of the revenue, even today.[49]

2.1 A Woman's Worth: Beauty Etiquette and Proper Femininity

Advertising reflects our values; in 1950, like today, cosmetic products and fashion advertisements were very prevalent, especially in women's magazines. Therefore, the number one target of these ads was women; the advertisements should reflect a woman's wants, needs, and beliefs. The "feminine douche" is an example of such a product for women, whose advertisement exemplifies women's worth. Figure 1 (see: Appendix A, p. 25), an advertisement for a hygiene product by the brand *Zonite*, published in 1950, presents a woman as "the problem". She is shown with a facial expression and gesture that convey anxiety and shame. The woman is blamed for her husband's frigidity; she is the problem of her marriage. Now that she has found the solution to what the advertisement names the "grave womanly offense", she regrets not having discovered it earlier. The caption below the picture reads: "Failure to practice hygiene [...] often results in such needless tragedies—homes broken up, few social invitations, the feeling of being shunned without knowing why". The product promises to solve all of a woman's problems, and to give her instant access to "health, married happiness" and social respectability, her three main concerns. Zonite is "Safe! Safe! Safe!" and can be used as often as needed because it is "so powerfully effective yet so harmless", so there remains no reason why any "modern woman" should not deliver those around her, especially her husband, from her bad-smelling burden. This advertisement exemplifies the idea that a woman will find her ultimate fulfillment in pleasing her husband and that she should feel guilty if she does not do her utmost to be as attractive and desirable as she possibly can. Even though vaginal douching was deemed unnecessary and even dangerous as early as 1911, the product was still advertised with high frequency.[50]

---

[49] see: Cortese, A., p. 27.
[50] Palmer, R. and Greenberg, S., "Facts and Frauds in Woman's Hygiene", *The Sun Dial Press*, New York 1936. *MUM.org: Museum of Menstruation and Women's Health* 2006, p. 142-149, 12 January 2009. <http://www.mum.org/facfraud3.htm>.

Advertisements for beauty and hygiene products, especially, present women with new ways to be beautiful and feminine, that she is obligated to try in order to be acceptable. An Advertisement from 1954, for *Halo*[51], a shampoo said to "glorify" hair, has a female character in a cartoon saying "even winning a song contest didn't make up for my gruesome looking hair". Therefore, no matter what other things a woman accomplishes, her worth is determined only by her looks. Figure 2 (see: Appendix A, p. 26) shows an advertisement for *Palmolive Soap,* published in 1950, that provides a list of which attributes comprise a feminine character. The wording "daintiness, purity, gentleness, mildness, loveliness" alongside little cheerful cherubs conveys the message that a woman should be exactly that, a little smiling, mild angel. Another *Palmolive Soap*[52] product carries the tagline "just for him", nicely summing up the purpose of all the beauty-hassle.

2.2 Women Portrayed as Inferior to Men

Instead of a career, women in the 1950s were constantly pursuing men; they dreamed of finding their ultimate fulfillment as wives, mothers and homemakers. Women put the needs of husband and family before anything else. Advertisement translates these feminine ambitions into women being more dependent, and even less intelligent, than their male counterpart. The advertisement for *Brillo Soap Pads* (see: Appendix A, figure 3, p. 26), from 1950, does exactly that. The woman pictured is "in tears over crusty pans", not exactly a problem to despair about, but that is the point: this woman has nothing more serious to deal with in her life, no more important decisions to make and her only real "job" is to clean the dirty dishes. Even this she failed at. The smiling woman in the second part of the advertisement, is just so happy about the major improvement in her life, made possible through *Brillo.* This goes on to show that women are very easily impressed and therefore less sophisticated than men, because of their limited horizons. The naïveté of women is again emphasized in the *Oneida Community Silverplate* advertisement of figure 4 (see: Appendix A, p. 27). The oversized picture shows a woman with an enamored expression on her made-up face, suggesting an overly feminine defenselessness. Pictured alongside her is a set of decorative spoons. In contrast to this is the much smaller picture in the bottom corner,

[51] "Halo Shampoo", Ad*Access On-Line Project, John W. Hartman Center for Sales, Advertising & Marketing History, *Duke University Rare Book, Manuscript, and Special Collections Library* 2007, 12 January 2009. <http://library.duke.edu/digitalcollections/adaccess.BH0459/>.
[52] "Palmolive Beauty Soap", Ad*Access On-Line Project, John W. Hartman Center for Sales, Advertising & Marketing History, *Duke University Rare Book, Manuscript, and Special Collections Library* 2007, 12 January 2009. <http://library.duke.edu/digitalcollections/adaccess.BH1064/>.

of her and a man, probably her husband, kissing. The copy reads, "she's in love…and she loves Community"; stating that this woman is actually in love with a set of silver cutlery, again depicts her as very easily amused. Her husband might receive the thankful kiss, but her real love is reserved for this "tarnish-resistant" silverware.

2.3 Women as Decorative Objects

Men in the 1950s adored women not for their brains, but for their beauty; women therefore did everything in their power to keep their beauty alive and thriving. Beautiful women presented an "eye-catcher" in any advertisement. "Sex sells" has become a popular idea in the late 20th century, but "sexual content in mass media has been around as long as mass media itself"[53]. Commonly the product has nothing to do with women, nudity or sex, but still, women's bodies are used to sell everything from shoe polish to trucks. Figure 5 (see: Appendix A, p. 28) shows a woman barely covered by fur, advertising *Griffin Microsheen* shoe polish. Her breasts are the first focal point of the advertisement, which sparks interest in the male observer and leaves him trying to locate the product that promises him this lady in reward for purchase. The text written on a scroll, which she holds in her hand reads her New Year's resolution, to "Trap me a man with a Microsheen Shine!" again enforcing the idea that any male who will use this product is the object of the attractive female's desire. In an *International Truck*[54] advertisement that ran during the 1940s and 50s, a young Marilyn Monroe look-alike in a bathing suit is pictured above the yellow company truck, holding a *Coca-Cola* bottle. The text reads "the girl delivers the message, *Internationals* deliver the goods", making it clear that the woman is only used to convey the product's excellence with her beauty. Her playful facial expression resonates innocence and plays on sexuality at the same time, making her attractive to a male audience and giving females the feeling that this is the appropriate way for them to look and act. Using a woman as a decorative object gives the impression that her character is subordinate to her outward appearance.

---

[53] Barker, F., "Sexual Messages in Advertising & Other Media", *Media Literacy Clearinghouse* 2008, 14 January 2008. <http://www.frankwbaker.com/sex_in_media.htm>.
[54] "International Trucks", 1940/50s, *Gallup & Robinson, Inc. for Advertising & Marketing Research*, 2009, 14 January 2009. <http://www.gallup-robinson.com/essayimages/10internationaltrucks.jpg>.

15

2.4 Women Portrayed as Housewives and Mothers

One of the most common stereotypes of women during the family-centered 1950s was the homemaker. Food, household and medical products are especially strong representatives of the stereotype, while advertisements concerning the care of children seem to view mothers as their only recipients. Headlines such as: "Mothers! Guard Against Those 'Dirt Danger' Days"[55], referring to children's dirty hands, sees women as the principle caretaker. Some go as far as even accusing mothers of neglect and mistakes: "Mother! Stop Neglecting 3 Flu or Cold Zones!"[56] and "How a Mother's Innocent Mistake Kept Her Child Pale and Tired for Years"[57]. The father is never tied into raising the children. Advertisements for household-, and especially cleaning-products, also address women almost exclusively. Women are to take care of the house and enjoy it, as the catchy phrase "Happy Housewives All Agree, Magic Nylif, that's for me!"[58], advertising a carpet sweeper, implies. A 1950 advertisement for *Hotpoint* dishwashers, shown in figure 6 (see: Appendix A, p. 29), shows a woman cleaning the dishes by hand, while her husband and children are watching TV in the living room. The "wall of dishes" that separates her from the rest of her family is a metaphor for a woman's sphere, in the kitchen. The text below reads, "Please...let your wife come into the living room! Don't let dirty dishes make your wife a kitchen exile"; it is implied that the husband be so gracious as to buy her a dishwasher, but does not suggest he take part in the work in any way. A TV commercial from 1952 for *Fab*[59] detergent presents the two sides of a story about dirty clothes. The man is shown first, saying "that's a woman for you, I asked her to get my shirts whiter, but does she call this whiter?" then switches over to the upset wife who laments "that's just like a man, how can I get his shirts as white as he wants?" But the *Fab* lady comes to the rescue, uniting "our friends" and, in the end, getting grumpy to say "boy really white shirts at last!" This again goes to show that women are simply expected to take care of the household and keep everything immaculate, if they do not, they will even be accused of not trying hard enough. While the husband from the *Fab* commercial might need his

[55] "Lava Soap", Ad*Access On-Line Project, John W. Hartman Center for Sales, Advertising & Marketing History, *Duke University Rare Book, Manuscript, and Special Collections Library* 2007, 12 January 2009. <http://library.duke.edu/digitalcollections/adaccess.BH1180/pg.1/>.
[56] "Super Anahist Cold Tablets", Ad*Access On-Line Project, John W. Hartman Center for Sales, Advertising & Marketing History, *Duke University Rare Book, Manuscript, and Special Collections Library* 2007, 12 January 2009. <http://library.duke.edu/digitalcollections/mma.MM0469/pg.1/>.
[57] "Kapsolvs Children's Vitamins", Ad*Access On-Line Project. John W. Hartman Center for Sales, Advertising & Marketing History, *Duke University Rare Book, Manuscript, and Special Collections Library* 2007, 12 January 2009. <http://library.duke.edu/digitalcollections/mma.MM0478/pg.1/>.
[58] "Magic Nylif", 1956, *Flickr, Yahoo* 2007, 18 January 2008. <http://www.flickr.com/photos/drewzel/2067751710/sizes/o/>.
[59] "Fab Detergent, 1952", *YouTube, LLC* 2008, 15 January 2009. <http://de.youtube.com/watch?v=SOOlcVAblEI>.

white shirts for work, the wife, in her apron is never portrayed as finding anything wrong with her role solely as housewife (if it was not for her peevish husband). The abundance of advertisements showing women as domestic goddesses, primped, pretty and satisfied wives and mothers, leaves us with the impression that women were simply not interested in a career.

2.5 Exclusively White

Aside from the widespread image of the young, fragile housewife, with the last thing on her mind probably being a job, another noticeable aspect of 1950s advertising is its exclusive "whiteness", its lack of racial diversity. Before the Civil Rights Movement, advertising was almost completely void of ethnic minorities. When they were pictured, it was in demeaning stereotypes; this was done to preserve the white feeling of "supremacy". The industry held an innate fear of loosing costumers when integrating minorities into the "average" white family picture.[60] A stereotype of African-American women, the "black mammy—subservient, dark, heavy, asexual, and inarticulate"[61] is dominant mainly in advertisings for food and beverages, reminiscent of the black family servant. *Aunt Jemima* is such a stereotype used to sell "heart-warmin' and happifyin'"[62] Pancakes, adding incorrect grammar to the list of stereotypical attributes.

3. Constructive Criticism

Criticism of gender stereotypes goes hand-in-hand with the women's movement. During the first wave, women criticized the existing beauty culture that pushed them to wear many layers of clothing, restricting movement. The second wave brought the emancipation of the housewife and the rebellion against instruments of male oppression, like make-up and high heels. And third wavers are continuing the fight against new impossible gender roles, such as the ideal for a woman to be extremely thin.[63]

Advertising's omnipresence and the evidence of a sexist society it provides, has made it a logical target for feminists, since the late 1960s.[64] They began to see advertising as

---

[60] see: Cortese, A., p. 91-93.
[61] ibid., p. 92.
[62] "Aunt Jemima Pancakes", 1950. *Gallup & Robinson, Inc. for Advertising & Marketing Research* 2007, 14 January 2009. <http://graphic-design.tjs-labs.com/show-picture?id=1185245047>.
[63] see: Dicker, R., p. 140-142.
[64] see: Craig, S., "Madison Avenue versus *The Feminine Mystique*: How the Advertising

a source of spreading unrealistic ideals and were determined to take action against the sexual stereotyping in magazines, newspapers, on television and the radio.[65] A group of activists called Media Women took action by posting stickers reading "this ad insults women", on offensive advertisements in public space.[66] After NOW announced that its members would "carry on a systematic boycott of products that in their advertising depict the woman as a supercilious idiot"[67], advertisers realized the urgent economic interest they had in responding to feminist concerns. "Revising advertising's image of women simply made good business sense"[68], but how this "new woman" wanted to be portrayed was unclear, even among feminists.[69] One aspect this image should definitely not include was the full-time housewife-stereotype present in most advertisements, even though 42% of women were part of the work force in the late 1960s.[70] A study of 1200 television commercials in 1973 shows that women were still portrayed in stereotypical, demeaning ways, despite the efforts of feminists: in 33.9% women were portrayed as dependent on men, in 17.1% they were portrayed as unintelligent, in 24.3% as submissive, in 37.5% as men's domestic adjuncts, in 22.7% as demeaned housekeepers, in 16.7% as sex objects, and in 42.6% as household functionaries.[71]

At the dawn of the new millennium, has not society moved beyond these sexist ideals of the past? Are the stereotypes of the 1950s still topical?

4. The Old New Thing: Advertising of the 1990s

The advertising industry experienced an unparalleled boom in the 1980s, with expenditures nearly doubled.[72] The "dot-com" hype of the 1990s added a new aspect to the industry: Internet advertising. The online sector of the industry grew quickly during the mid-1990s, but remained limited until the new millennium, due to the uncertainty of the new technology. [73]

Industry Responded to the Onset of the Modern Women's Movement", *The Annenberg School for Communication at University of Pennsylvania* 2006, 30 December 2008.
<http://www.asc.upenn.edu/courses/comm334/Docs/femads.pdf>.
[65] see: Davis, F., p. 109-110.
[66] see: Dicker, R., p. 141.
[67] Craig, S., p. 4.
[68] ibid., p. 4.
[69] see: ibid., p. 6.
[70] see: Davis, F., p. 110.
[71] Fischer-Hornung, D., Women in the USA, Bayerischer Schulbuch-Verlag, Munich, Germany 1991, p. 13.
[72] see: Cortese, A., p. 4.
[73] "The Internet Links the World", *Thinkquest* 1999, 21 January 2009.
<http://www.library.thinkquest.org/27629/themes/media/md90s.html>.

The focus of advertising remains on printed media, as Internet advertising made for only 3% of the total spending on advertising.[74]

4.1 Sky-High Beauty Ideal

Women were still the number one consumers in the 1990s with 70-80% of products being purchased by women.[75] However, this new generation of customers is better educated and more sophisticated than their foremothers. With women being more involved in society, economy and politics, advertising should reflect these changed times. But that is the problem; the advertising industry displays women the way that is economically most profitable for it. If the beauty ideal set for women is almost impossible to live up to, they will continue to buy products, trying to achieve this goal. Beauty ideals have become even more unattainable in the age of digital retouching; even if in the 1950s women were polished and pampered, the work that could be done to photographs was limited and the costumer could rely on the fact that what they saw was a real person. Computerized images allow advertisers to compile multiple faces and bodies, selecting only the most beautiful traits, thereby creating a new "cyber woman", non-existent in the real world. Stick-thin women with big breasts, luscious hair and flawless (even pore-less) skin promise that any woman can look like them, if she only buys this product.

On the other hand, there is also improvement. It is conveyed to the woman of the 1990s that she is not doing all this for a man, but for herself. L'Oréal's famous slogan "Because I'm worth it"[76], expresses this emancipated sentiment. Any excuse is given to use the product, which does not imply the male benefit. In a commercial for *Bongo Jeans*[77] from 1997, a beautiful young woman is used to deliver the message that fashion is fun. She is shown making faces, striking poses, laughing and joking around. Her carefree behavior shows that she has moved beyond the strict behavior code set for women in the 1950s. Despite emancipated women claiming to have fun with fashion and beauty, advertisers promote an image of women that implies only tall, young, and extremely thin women are beautiful. Some advertisers have responded to this trend, of

[74] "Figure 9: Internet as a Portion of Total Advertising (1999)", Chart, *Classicbranding.com*, 22 Jan. 2009 <http://www.internet-advertising-ia.com/Internet_Advertising/ Advertising_8.htm>.
[75] Waters, J. and Ellis, G., "The Selling of Gender Identity" in: Advertising and Culture, Cross, K. (ed), Praeger, Westport, Connecticut 1996, p. 93.
[76] "Because I'm Worth It: The Story Behind the Legendary Phrase", *L'Oréal Paris*, 21 January 2009. <http://www.lorealparisusa.com/_us/_en/default.aspx#page=top{nav|media:_blank|overlay:worthit|diagnostic|main:about|userdata}>.
[77] "Bongo Jeans", 1997. *YouTube, LLC* 2008. 19 January 2009. <http://de.youtube.com/watch?v=7BVpp-9Pmlk&feature=related>.

promoting an unhealthy body image, with counter campaigns. *The Body Shop*, known for its community service and global activism, also targeted a change in the beauty culture. An advertisement for their company (see: Appendix A, figure 7, p. 29) shows a buxom parody of the *Barbie* doll. The copy reads "there are 3 billion women who don't look like supermodels and only 8 who do", giving the hint that the ideals portrayed are nowhere close to reality. A series of *Kellogg's Special K* advertisements[78] aired in 1996, with the slogan "look good on your own terms", promoting a healthy way of defining beauty. One advertisement features a woman in her fifties with her arms around two African women standing on either side of her and the text "the Ashantis of Ghana think a woman's body gets more attractive as she ages. Please contact your travel agent for the next available flight". The use of humor and puns is noticeable and suggests a light-hearted approach to this difficult topic.

The Body Shop and *Special K* advertisements go to show that there is a divide about the image of women promoted. Are they acceptable even if they are not a size zero? If searching for the answer to this question by flipping through a magazine from the 1990s, sadly it would still be 'no'; a woman must be thin, young, and flawless in order to be attractive and socially acceptable.

4.2 Women in Relation to Men

The definition of what is "politically correct" to show in an advertisement has changed since the 1950s. Women are not shown as supercilious idiots too embarrassed to ask for a box of tampons at the drug store anymore. Especially the sexual revolution gave women a new confidence in themselves. But what was once an obvious display of male superiority has moved to a more subconscious level. An advertisement for *Escape* perfume for men by Calvin Klein (see: Appendix A, figure 8, p. 30) illustrates this idea. The man is hovering above the woman, looking down on her, while she stretches her neck to reach up to him. The woman looks helpless and in need of the man's protection. In contrast, other companies have sought to catch up with feminist ideology and display women with a new confidence. One famous example is the advertising campaign for *Virginia Slims* cigarettes, introduced in 1968. Their slogan "you've come a long way baby", which was also made into a jingle, speaks to the emancipated, empowered woman. The advertisements show anecdotes of women's oppression, such as having to do all the housework and being punished for smoking,

---

[78] "Kellogg's Special K", 1996, *Media Awareness Network*, 18 January 2009. <http://www.reseau-medias.ca/english/resources/educational/handouts/advertising_marketing/special_k_ad_6.cfm>.

and contrasts these with images of the glamorous "new woman". An example from the 1990s (see: Appendix A, figure 9, p. 31) shows an attractive, smiling, confident woman, putting on sturdy boots, looking like she is ready for adventure. The copy reads, "We know a woman is perfectly capable of doing anything a man can. The question is, why would she want to?" which refers to the small picture in the corner of a man being shot from a cannon. The advertisement bluntly states the egalitarianism as a universally accepted truth and even goes as far as asking why women should be satisfied with doing the things men do, why should they not invent new things for themselves? While the pro-feminist *Virginia Slims* campaign can be seen as just another marketing strategy, it nonetheless makes a statement important for women's advance.

Again a split can be seen in the advertisements: on the one hand, women are subtly portrayed as inferior to men, but on the other hand, women are also shown as liberated and in charge of their lives.

4.3 Oversexed and Underage

While in the 1950s, women might have been used as pretty decoration in an advertisement, this idea was radicalized, in the 1990s, to the extent of female hypersexualisation and fragmentation of the body. The use of bare skin in advertising during the 1950s was mostly limited to products where it was necessary to show women with less clothing, such as lingerie. Even when women were used merely as objects of desire, sexuality not being related to the product, the use of skin was modest, exposing limited cleavage at most. The change in this stereotypical portrayal of women provides evidence of drastic social change. With the sexual revolution and the age of the hippie, taboos were broken and nudity became more widely accepted. This also increased the use of sexuality in advertising, shown by the incline of sexual explicitness (defined as kissing, hugging and the depiction or suggestion of sexual activity) by 32% in only a decade, from 1983 to 1993.[79] Figure 10 (see: Appendix A, p. 32) shows an advertisement for *Obsession* cologne by *Calvin Klein*, published in 1994. The model is Kate Moss, shown facing the camera, with her breasts completely exposed. The expression on her face does not exude confidence, but more a feeling of suspicion, while her hand in front of her mouth symbolizes her weakness and silence. As she is used to advertise a product for men, the intention of the advertiser is clear, the implied message being that this beauty will be waiting for you, in this pose, if only

---

[79] "Advertising Is More Sexually Explicit, Researchers Say", *University of North Texas News Service* 1999, 10 January 2009. <http://web3.unt.edu/news/story.cfm?story=7429>.

you buy this product. The product name "obsession" can also be understood as a label for the woman; she is the thing, which the man desires and hunts for. The negative connotation of the word can make this quite intimidating to a woman.

The advertising industry uses sexual explicitness to attract attention. In order to keep rousing the same amount of attention, they have to break more and more taboos, constantly challenging the limits of sex in advertising. Just how much further could one go than showing a completely nude woman's upper body? Well, you could introduce violence, such as an advertisement for *Fetish* perfume[80] did. This particular advertisement features a young woman with a perfume bottle tucked into her bikini top and the copy "apply generously to your neck so he can smell the scent as you shake your head 'no'". Implying that a woman does not mean the words she says reads like an open invitation for sexual harassment and is very demeaning at least. If implied violence did not cause the hoped-for interest, maybe featuring underage models will. A series of advertisements from 1995, by the notorious *Calvin Klein,* features teenage models around the age of fifteen or sixteen, in suggestive poses. One shows a young girl with her finger in her mouth, lying provocatively on her back, allowing the viewer a straight look between her legs at her white cotton underwear.[81] In the 1950s a young woman would not have been caught dead wearing something this revealing, let alone pose in such an unladylike position. The feeling of innocence that was so often hinted at in advertisements back then is lost in the direct address of the viewer; in the 1990s, the hypersexualisation jumps out of the picture.

Fragmentation of the female body means focusing only on one part of a woman, or even detaching it completely. Advertisers use this to their advantage, by borrowing only the most appealing parts, most often breasts, as Figure 11 (see: Appendix A, p. 33) shows. This advertisement for *Icebreakers* chewing gum obviously tried to use sex appeal to their advantage and make their ordinary product more extraordinary. Trying to incorporate humor as well as sex, an unbeatable combination, the advertisement links a woman's aroused nipple to their new "cool" chewing gum, again a double entendre. But focusing just on one part of a woman does not only convey that her character is of no interest, but actually makes her even less than human. Not only is she an object, she is just part of that object.

---

[80] Simon, C., "Hooked on Advertising", *Ms. Magazine Online* 2000, 21 January 2009.
<http://www.msmagazine.com/jan01/hooked2_jan01.html>.
[81] "Calvin Klein Jeans", 1995, *The Mongoose Eats at Midnight* 2007, 21 January 2009
<http://chelseakissell.blogspot.com/2007/04/sex-appeal-much.html>.

4.4 Housewife Turned Superwoman

The mindless stereotype of the happy housewife, received a makeover during the last four decades. She is now more confident, receives help from her male counterpart and is promised equal job opportunity. The labor force participation rate for women saw a major increase of 42.3% from 1950 to 1998.[82] Advertisers have shifted more towards reflecting the realistic ambitions of women, outside the home. A 1999 advertisement for a recruiting agency (see: Appendix A, figure 12 p. 33) pictures a urinal and text reading, "this is the only place a woman can't reach in a company". Laid out to attract female applicants, this advertisement assures of the unlimited opportunity offered to women in their company.

Concerning the function of mother and caretaker, advertising remains "focused on [women's] responsibility for caring for others"[83], because this will push women continually to buy food, household, healthcare and beauty products in order to perform her "job" adequately. However, a shift toward a more "politically correct" tone is noticeable. It has become socially unacceptable to make women the only ones responsible for the household. An advertisement for a 1999 *Zanussi* washing machine (see: Appendix A, figure 13, p. 34) cleverly incorporates the male into doing chores. "Bi-sexual washing machines. So easy to use that even man can", the copy reads, accompanied by the universal symbol for female and male, joint together and made to look like a washing machine door. The advertising industry has tried to make their products more gender neutral, with the economic aspect of reaching more costumers. They also try to avoid addressing only the mother of a child, concerning healthcare, food and other products directed at upholding the family health and happiness. The housewife has turned into a more confident, modern superwoman, handling her child on one arm, while balancing her paper work on the other.

4.5 Diversity

Probably one of the most positive developments of the way advertising portrays women is the inclusion of other races, nationalities, and sexual orientations. The Civil Rights Movement, as well as lesbian activism during the second and third wave of feminism, addressed the issues of minorities and drastically changed their social status. Interracial friendships are shown more often, especially in products targeted at women,

---

[82] "Changes in Women's Labor Force Participation in the 20th Century", *U.S. Bureau of Labor Statistics* 2000, 21 January 2009. <http://www.bls.gov/opub/ted/2000/feb/wk3/art03.htm>.
[83] Parkin, K., p. 30.

such as cosmetics and feminine hygiene. References to female homosexuality can also be found more frequently in advertising; however, this concept is sometimes exploited on the basis of sexual fantasies, love not being part of the essential message.

IV. Conclusion

Advertising sells more than a product, it sells ideals. It tries to tell us who we are and who we should be; it defines what it means to be a woman. If one tried to describe the position of women by looking at advertisements from the 1950s, the message would be first and foremost, housewife and mother. In addition, characteristics such as pretty, primped, feminine, caring, loving, and docile would probably be listed. This description reflects women's social status during the conservative era. A woman's place was believed to be in the home and every female's aspiration was to ultimately fulfill her "suburban dream" of house, husband and children. How do the 1990s compare? The beauty industry still plays upon women's need to fulfill the ideal, which changed from a more curvaceous body of the 1950s to an almost emaciated thinness, and demands computerized perfection. But judging from television and print advertising, there has also been some improvement; women managed to leave the home, and are granted wider access to a career. Women's status has also been promoted in society; even though she had achieved legal equality long before the 1990s, only the "personal is political" agenda of the second wave of feminism incorporated this egalitarianism into their private lives. The "glass ceiling", limiting the housewife, was shattered and new doors opened. However, the problem with stereotypes is that as soon as one becomes obsolete, another jumps in to fill the empty space. Just why are stereotypes so persistent? Why have they survived every update? Our fast-paced world forces us to make quick decisions, so men and women alike try to simplify the process and turn to experts for patterns to bring fast success, every time. "Commercials appear to do just that; they give us the one-minute solution."[84] Advertisers have, however, realized that a more sophisticated audience will no longer accept mindless stereotyping, and try to adapt. They do this by basically employing two strategies; the first is to simply reverse gender roles, thereby emphasizing the concept of universal interchangeability of said roles. The second, more complex strategy is to incorporate the "new woman" image into advertising, as in the *Virginia Slims* campaign. The explicit references to feminism, these advertisements make, show that the idea of equality for women is not as natural yet as maybe it should be. One of the most positive changes over the past 40 years is

---

[84] Waters, J. and Ellis, G., p. 95.

the increasing acknowledgement of the diversity of women, beginning to be reflected in advertising. The integration of ethnic minorities and sexual orientations other than heterosexuality is becoming more prominent, however, there remains room for improvement, as stereotypes prevail. The "superwoman", who handles it all, career, children, and household, as well as the hypersexualised "femme fatale", using her beauty and body to sell almost anything, are two stereotypes that developed out of shifted gender relations and a more competitive market. Does this mean that, to retain shock value, the exploitation of women and their bodies, for the sake of sale, will only increase? The effect of the ever more demanding beauty ideals on body image are commonly focused on in the 21st century; studies show that 78% of 17-year-olds are dissatisfied with their body and that 75% of women are "more afraid of spending a day at the beach in a thong than of having a root canal at the dentist"[85]. Even though the second statement might seem humorous, the underlying concern is serious, because in many cases, being dissatisfied with one's body, leads to harmful dieting, eating disorders and unnecessary plastic surgery. The media and advertising in particular are continually blamed for feeding women with images harmful to their self-esteem. The 2008 headline "EU Parliament Calls for Less Sexism in Advertising"[86], goes to show that North America is not the only one with a problem. As solutions for improvement are sought after it is important to remember that progress has been made. "It is wrong to assert that corporate America has been unresponsive to feminism. On the contrary, it has responded in its own predictable fashion"[87], but not enough, in feminists' opinion. Advertising is a double-edged sword; it is the lifeblood of economy, but the death of our individuality. The difficulty of making it more human and more representative of reality is convincing managers that showing women as multifaceted beings will not ruin their monthly paycheck.

---

[85] "'The Body Project' to offer a dramatic look at body-image obsession of today's woman", *The Ithaca Journal,* Theithacajournal.com 22 January 2009, 23 January 2009.
<http://www.theithacajournal.com/article/20090122/ENTERTAINMENT03/901220313>.
[86] "EU Parliament Calls for Less Sexism in Advertising", *Spiegel Online International,* Spiegelnet GMBH 3 September 2008, 23 January 2009.
<http://www.spiegel.de/international/europe/0,1518,576117,00.html>.
[87] Barthel, D., p. 124.

25

V. Appendix

A. Print Advertisements

Figure 1: "Zonite Feminine Douche", Ad*Access On-Line Project, John W. Hartman Center for Sales, Advertising & Marketing History, *Duke University Rare Book, Manuscript, and Special Collections Library* 2007, 12 January 2009. <http://library.duke.edu/digitalcollections/adaccess.BH0213/>.

Figure 2: "Palmolive Beauty Soap", Ad*Access On-Line Project, John W. Hartman Center for Sales, Advertising & Marketing History, *Duke University Rare Book, Manuscript, and Special Collections Library* 2007, 12 January 2009. <http://library.duke.edu/digitalcollections/adaccess.BH1118/>.

Figure 3: "Brillo Soap Pads", <u>Woman's Day</u> 01 February 1950, *Gallery of Graphic Design* 2007, 13 January 2009. <http://graphic-design.tjs-labs.com/show-picture?id=1184879398>.

Figure 4: "Oneida Community Silverplate", <u>Life</u> 19 October 1953, *Gallery of Graphic Design* 2007, 13 January 2009. <http://www.graphic-design.tjs-labs.com/show-picture?id=1170281098>.

Figure 5: "Griffin Microsheen", 1957, *Found in Mom's Basement* 2008, 14 January 2009.
<http://www.pzrservices.typepad.com/vintageadvertising/vintage_sexist_advertising/>.

Figure 6: "Hotpoint Dishwashers", 1950, *Found in Mom's Basement* 2007, 15 January 2009. <http://www.pzrservices.typepad.com/vintageadvertising/vintage_sexist_advertising/page/4/>.

Figure 7: "The Body Shop", Addressing Body Image, Self-Esteem, and Eating Disorders, *EGallery* 2001, 22 Jan. 2009.
<http://www.ucalgary.ca/~egallery/volume2/small.html>.

Figure 8: "Escape by Calvin Klein", <u>Harpers Bazaar</u> 1993, *Gallup & Robinson, Inc.*, 22 January 2009. <http://www.gallup-robinson.com/essay40.html>.

Figure 9: "Virginia Slims", 1991, *Tobacco Documents Online*, 22 January 2009.
<http://tobaccodocuments.org/pollay_ads/Virg01.05b.html?ocr_position=hide_ocr>.

Figure 10: "Obsession by Calvin Klein", <u>Cosmopolitan</u> 1994, *Gallup & Robinson, Inc.*,
22 January 2009. <http://www.gallup-robinson.com/essay67.html>.

Figure 11: "Icebreakers Chewing Gum", 1999, *AdMe.ru*, 22 January 2009.
<http://www.adme.ru/paedia/prints/1999/01/11/8169/>.

Figure 12: "Women's Employment", 1999, *AdMe.ru*, 22 January 2009.
<http://www.adme.ru/paedia/prints/1999/02/24/9102/>.

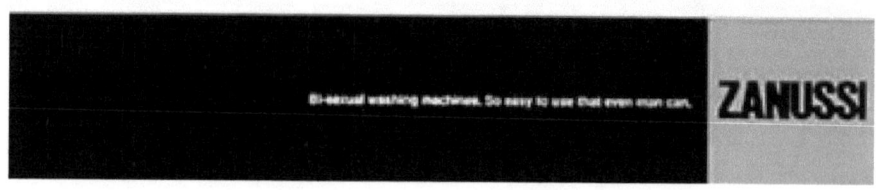

Figure 13: "Zanussi Washing Machine", 1999, *AdMe.ru,* 22 January 2009.
<http://www.adme.ru/paedia/prints/1999/11/09/14524/>.

B. Bibliography

Books

Barth, M., <u>Stark reduziert!</u>, Silke Schreiber Verlag, Heidenheim an der Brenz, Germany 2000.

Berkeley, K., <u>The Women's Liberation Movement in America</u>, Greenwood Press, Westport, Connecticut 1999.

Cortese, A., <u>Provocateur: Images of Women and Minorities in Advertising</u>, Rowan & Littlefield Publishers, Inc., Lanham, Maryland 2008[3].

Davis, F., <u>Moving the Mountain: The Women's Movement in America since 1960</u>, Touchstone, New York 1991.

Dicker, R., <u>A History of U.S. Feminisms</u>, Seal Press, Berkeley, California 2008.

Fischer-Hornung, D., <u>Women in the USA</u>, Bayerischer Schulbuch-Verlag, Munich, Germany 1991.

Kroløkke, C. and Sørensen, A., <u>Gender Communication Theories & Analyses: From Silence to Performance</u>, Sage Publications, Thousand Oaks, California 2006.

Parkin, K., <u>Food Is Love: Food Advertising and Gender Roles in Modern America</u>, University of Pennsylvania Press, Philadelphia, Pennsylvania 2006.

Ryan, B., <u>Feminism and the Women's Movement</u>, Routledge, New York 1992.

Sochen, J., <u>Movers and Shakers: American Women Thinkers and Activists 1900-1970</u>, Quadrangle, New York 1973.

Waters, J. and Ellis, G., "The Selling of Gender Identity" in: <u>Advertising and Culture</u>, Cross, K. (ed), Praeger, Westport, Connecticut 1996.

Chart

"Figure 9: Internet as a Portion of Total Advertising (1999)", *Classicbranding.com*, 22 Jan. 2009 <http://www.internet-advertising-ia.com/Internet_Advertising/ Advertising_8.htm>.

Internet Articles

"Advertising", Def. 1, *The American Heritage® Dictionary of the English Language*, 4th ed., Houghton Mifflin, Boston 2000, 10 January 2009. <http://www.bartleby.com/61/57/A0105700.html>.

"Advertising Is More Sexually Explicit, Researchers Say", *University of North Texas News Service* 1999, 10 January 2009. <http://www.web3.unt.edu/news/story.cfm?story=7429>.

Barker, F., "Sexual Messages in Advertising & Other Media", *Media Literacy Clearinghouse* 2008, 14 January 2009. <http://www.frankwbaker.com/sex_in_media.htm>.

"Because I'm Worth It: The Story Behind the Legendary Phrase", *L'Oréal Paris*, 21 January 2009. <http://www.lorealparisusa.com/_us/_en/default.aspx#page= top{nav|media:_blank|overlay:worthit|diagnostic|main:about|userdata}>.

Boham L. and Lipton, M., "Women Writing: 1890-Present", *Yale-New Haven Teachers Institute* 2008, 23 December 2008. <http://www.yale.edu/ynhti/curriculum/units/1978/3/78.03.09.x.html>.

"Changes in Women's Labor Force Participation in the 20th Century", *U.S. Bureau of Labor Statistics* 2000, 21 Jan. 2009 <http://www.bls.gov/opub/ted/2000/feb/wk3/art03.htm>.

Craig, S., "Madison Avenue versus *The Feminine Mystique*: How the Advertising Industry Responded to the Onset of the Modern Women's Movement", *The Annenberg School for Communication at University of Pennsylvania* 2006, 30 December 2008. <http://www.asc.upenn.edu/courses/comm334/Docs/femads.pdf>.

Eisenberg, B. and Ruthsdotter, M., "Living the Legacy: The Women's Rights Movement 1848-1998", *National Women's History Project,* 28 December 2008. <http://www.legacy98.org/move-hist.html>.

"EU Parliament Calls for Less Sexism in Advertising", *Spiegel Online International,* Spiegelnet GMBH 3 September 2008, 23 January 2009. <http://www.spiegel.de/international/europe/0,1518,576117,00.html>.

"Highlights of Women's Earnings in 2007", *U.S. Bureau of Labor Statistics* 2007. 16 January 2009. <http://www.bls.gov/cps/cpswom2007.pdf>.

"Letter from Abigail Adams to John Adams, 31 March – April 1776", Adams Family Papers: An Electronic Archive, *Massachusetts Historical Society*, 18 December 2008. <http://www.masshist.org/digitaladams/aea/cfm/doc.cfm?id=L17760331aa>.

"Media Stereotyping", *Media Awareness Network* 2009, 11 January 2009. <http://www.media-awareness.ca/english/issues/stereotyping/>.

Palmer, R. and Greenberg, S., "Facts and Frauds in Woman's Hygiene", *The Sun Dial Press*, New York 1936. *MUM.org: Museum of Menstruation and Women's Health* 2006, p. 142-149, 12 January 2009. <http://www.mum.org/facfraud3.htm>.

Simon, C., "Hooked on Advertising", *Ms. Magazine Online* 2000, 21 January 2009. <http://www.msmagazine.com/jan01/hooked2_jan01.html>.

Stanton, E. and Mott, L. "The First Convention Ever Called to Discuss the Civil and Political Rights of Women, Seneca Falls, N.Y., July 19, 20, 1848", National American Woman Suffrage Association Collection, *Library of Congress,* 25 December 2008. <http://www.hdl.loc.gov/loc.rbc/rbnawsa.n7548>.

"'The Body Project' to offer a dramatic look at body-image obsession of today's woman", *The Ithaca Journal*, Theithacajournal.com 22 January 2009, 23 January 2009. <http://www.theithacajournal.com/article/20090122/ENTERTAINMENT 03/901220313>.

"The Internet Links the World", *Thinkquest* 1999, 21 January 2009. <http://www.library.thinkquest.org/27629/themes/media/md90s.html>.

Print Advertisements

Ad*Access On-Line Project, John W. Hartman Center for Sales, Advertising & Marketing History, *Duke University Rare Book, Manuscript, and Special Collections Library* 2007, 12 January 2009. <http://www.library.duke.edu/digitalcollections/adaccess/>.

AdMe.ru, 22 January 2009. <http://www.adme.ru>.

"Calvin Klein Jeans", 1995, *The Mongoose Eats at Midnight* 2007, 21 January 2009. <http://www.chelseakissell.blogspot.com/2007/04/sex-appeal-much.html>.

Found in Mom's Basement 2008, 14 January 2009. <http://www.pzrservices.typepad.com/vintageadvertising/vintage_sexist_advertising/>.

Gallery of Graphic Design 2007, 13 January 2009. <http://www.graphic-design.tjs-labs.com/>.

Gallup & Robinson, Inc. for Advertising & Marketing Research 2009, 14 January 2009. <http://www.gallup-robinson.com>.

"Kellogg's Special K", 1996, *Media Awareness Network* 1996, 18 January 2009. <http://www.reseau-medias.ca/english/resources/educational/handouts/advertising_marketing/special_k_ad_6.cfm>.

"Magic Nylif", 1956, *Flickr, Yahoo* 2007, 18 January 2008. <http://www.flickr.com/photos/drewzel/2067751710/sizes/o/>.

"The Body Shop", Addressing Body Image, Self-Esteem, and Eating Disorders, *EGallery* 2001, 22 January 2009. <http://www.ucalgary.ca/~egallery/volume2/small.html>.

"Virginia Slims", 1991, *Tabacco Documents Online* 1991, 22 January 2009. <http://www.tobaccodocuments.org/pollay_ads/Virg01.05b.html?ocr_position=hide_ocr>.

Television Commercials

"Fab Detergent", 1952, *YouTube, LLC* 2008, 15 January 2009. <http://de.youtube.com/watch?v=SOOlcVAblEl>.

"Bongo Jeans", 1997, *YouTube, LLC* 2008, 19 January 2009. <http://de.youtube.com/watch?v=7BVpp-9Pmlk&feature=related>.